ANIMALS of the DESERT

By Maggie Palmer
Illustrated by James Needham

Macmillan
McGraw-Hill

New York   Farmington

What do you think about when you think about the desert? That it's nothing but sand? Hot? Dry? Lifeless?

Deserts can be hot: some are the hottest places on earth. And they are dry. In some deserts, no rain comes down for years. But are deserts lifeless?

A desert is a place where little or no rain falls. The heat during the day can dry up the rain before it falls all the way to the ground.

But even the hottest desert can be very cold at night, because there are no clouds to hold in the day's heat.

Some deserts are covered by
sand dunes. Wind shapes the
sand into these rounded mounds.
In some places, sand dunes
spread out all around, as far as
you can see.

When the wind blows the sand just above the ground, the sand can pound against the desert rocks. That's how they get their weird shapes.

In such a hot, dry place, life is hard. But animals do live in the desert. They have to find special ways of keeping cool and finding enough water.

Snakes are cold-blooded. This means that they take on the temperature of their surroundings. Desert snakes like it hot. But even they have to find shade when the sun and sand are at their hottest.

Lizards are cold-blooded, too. Most lizards can't take as much heat as snakes, so they are always on the lookout for shade.

The dune lizard makes its own shade by holding its feet up, one at a time, until the sand covered by its shadow has cooled. Then it rests on the cooled sand with all four legs in the air.

Many animals hide underground
in holes during the day. They
come out at night to look for
food.

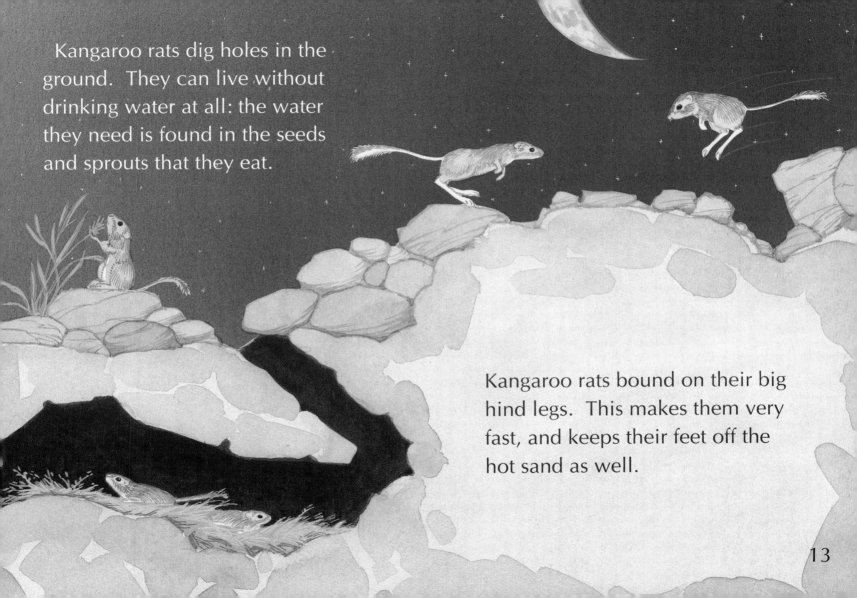

Kangaroo rats dig holes in the ground. They can live without drinking water at all: the water they need is found in the seeds and sprouts that they eat.

Kangaroo rats bound on their big hind legs. This makes them very fast, and keeps their feet off the hot sand as well.

13

Desert foxes have large ears so they can hear the sound of a mouse or other prey. Their ears keep them cool, too, with many blood vessels close to the skin so the wind can cool their blood.

Feathers protect desert birds from the sun. But they still need water. The male sand grouse has feathers like a sponge. He can soak them in water and carry the water back to his family that way.

Life in the desert has special problems. But many animals have found special ways of their own to survive there.